THE SOCIAL INNOVATIONS *LAB FRAMEWORK*

from idea exploration to execution

Tine Hansen-Turton
Nicholas Torres

SOCIAL INNOVATIONS
INSTITUTE

The *Social Innovations Institute & Lab* ™
Practical Education to Inspire an Entrepreneurial Mindset

The *Social Innovations Institute & Lab* ™ (www.socialinnovationslab.org) takes both emerging and established leaders and their companies through a process of innovation that transforms them into sharper, smarter and better versions of themselves.

Our **mission** is to help people, managers, leaders and their teams think in innovative ways to lead and redefine their respective industries. Our **philosophy** is about inspiring people and tapping into their values, passions, and culture to truly make a difference.

The *Social Innovations Institute & Lab* ™ approach takes teams through an innovation process from idea exploration through testing to plan execution. Our process will hone entrepreneurial and innovative thinking skills while developing, and eventually executing new or improved business innovations/models. We believe that the strongest ideas are created through a cross-disciplinary process, and that these ideas will take root, attract the needed capital and ultimately have a significant impact regionally, nationally, and globally.

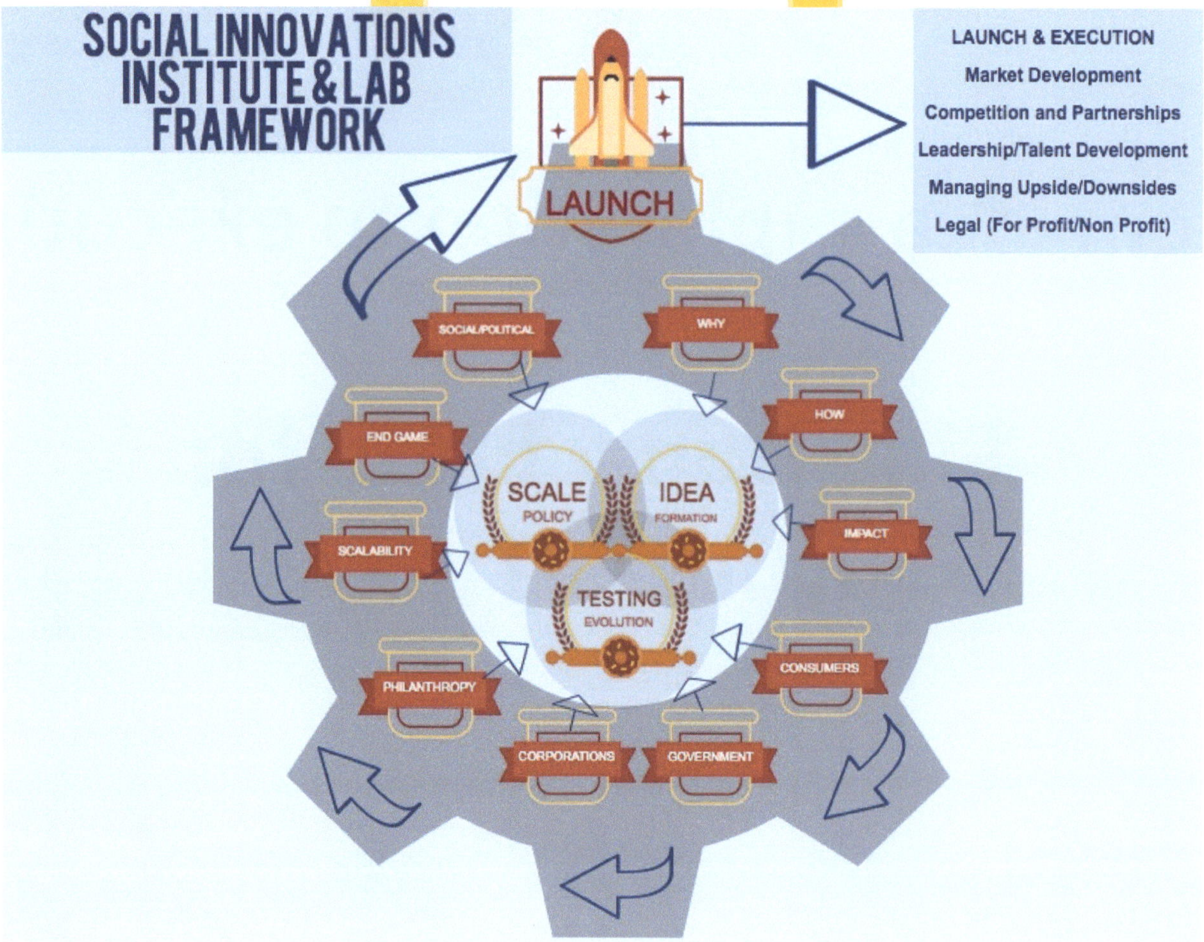

SOCIAL INNOVATIONS INSTITUTE & LAB FRAMEWORK

LAUNCH

LAUNCH & EXECUTION
Market Development
Competition and Partnerships
Leadership/Talent Development
Managing Upside/Downsides
Legal (For Profit/Non Profit)

SOCIAL/POLITICAL

WHY

HOW

END GAME

SCALE
POLICY

IDEA
FORMATION

IMPACT

SCALABILITY

TESTING
EVOLUTION

PHILANTHROPY

CONSUMERS

CORPORATIONS

GOVERNMENT

PROVEN SUCCESS

Piloted and tested at the University of Pennsylvania's Fels Institute of Government, the *Social Innovations Institute & Lab ™* framework is built on the premise that innovation is a process, not just an end result. Funded by the Robert Wood Johnson Foundation, Knight Foundation and the E. Rhodes and Leona B. Carpenter Foundation, the *Social Innovations Institute & Lab ™* has achieved tremendous results since it was launched. **500 ideas were sourced; 83 ideas were incubated; 51 Social Sector Businesses/Ideas (50% not for profit and 50% for profits) were launched (26) or launching (25) within Health (35%); Education (15%); Food (13%); Human Services (13%); Technology (9%) and Other Industries representing media, fair trade, veterans, and legal (15%).**

Social Innovations Institute & Lab ™ **resulted in $38,575,500 leveraged/earned between 2013-2016 and an expected additional $56,152,500 expected from 2016-2019 AND The Social Innovations Institute & Lab resulted in the creation of 372 jobs.**

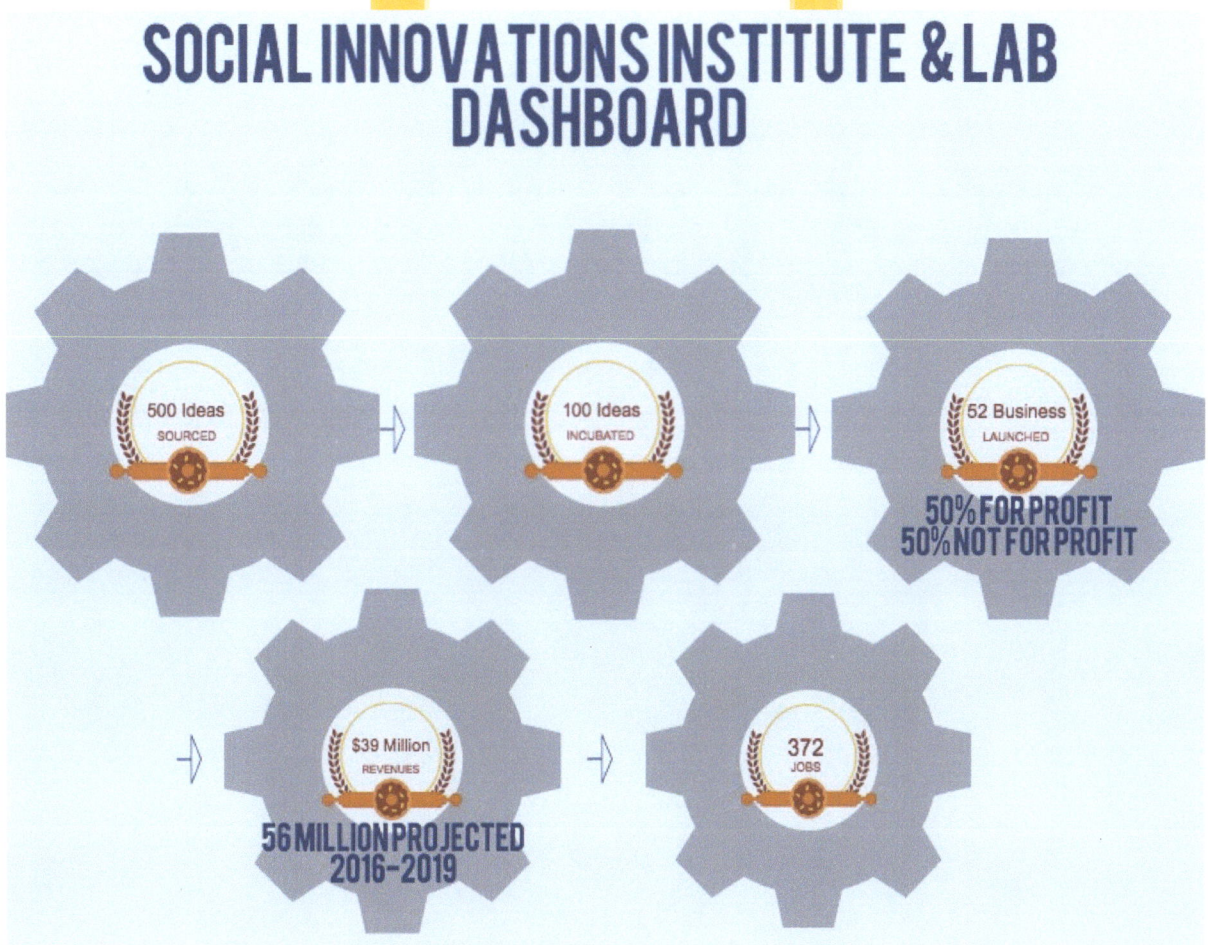

3

Social Innovations Institute & Lab ™ resulted in increased Social Innovation and Enterprise competencies in measuring Social Impact, an Innovative Mindset, Financial Modeling and Sustainability; Scaling and End Game Strategies, Creating Effective Marketing/Pitch Materials; Developing Markets, and Identifying and Addressing Social/Political Barriers.

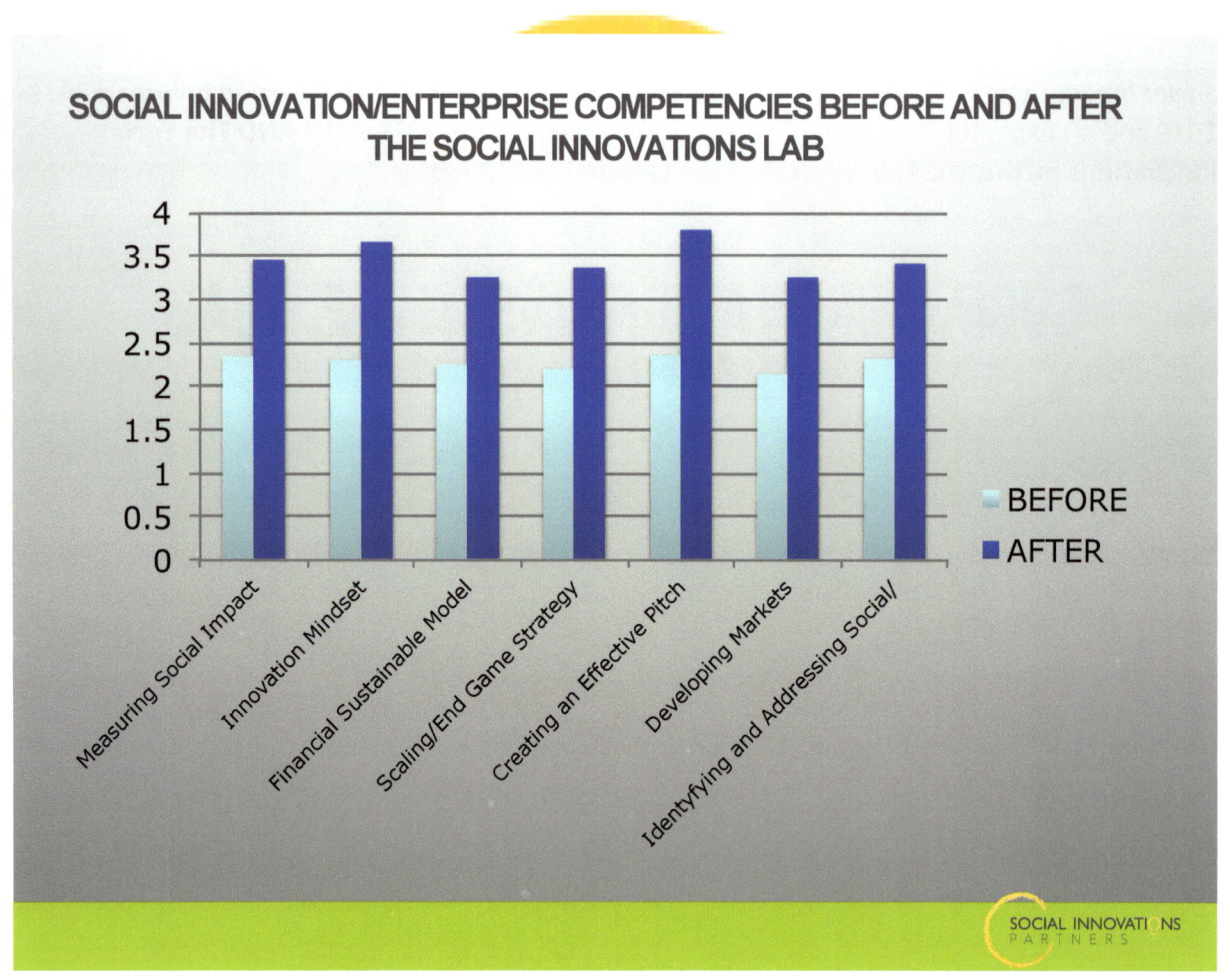

The *Social Innovations Institute & Lab ™* promotes innovative thinking by educating participants, providing opportunities for collaboration and networking, working with participants to find compelling evidence of their innovation's potential outcome, and providing the connection to mentors and potential financing. As explained in further detail in this document, the concepts covered over the course of the program include:

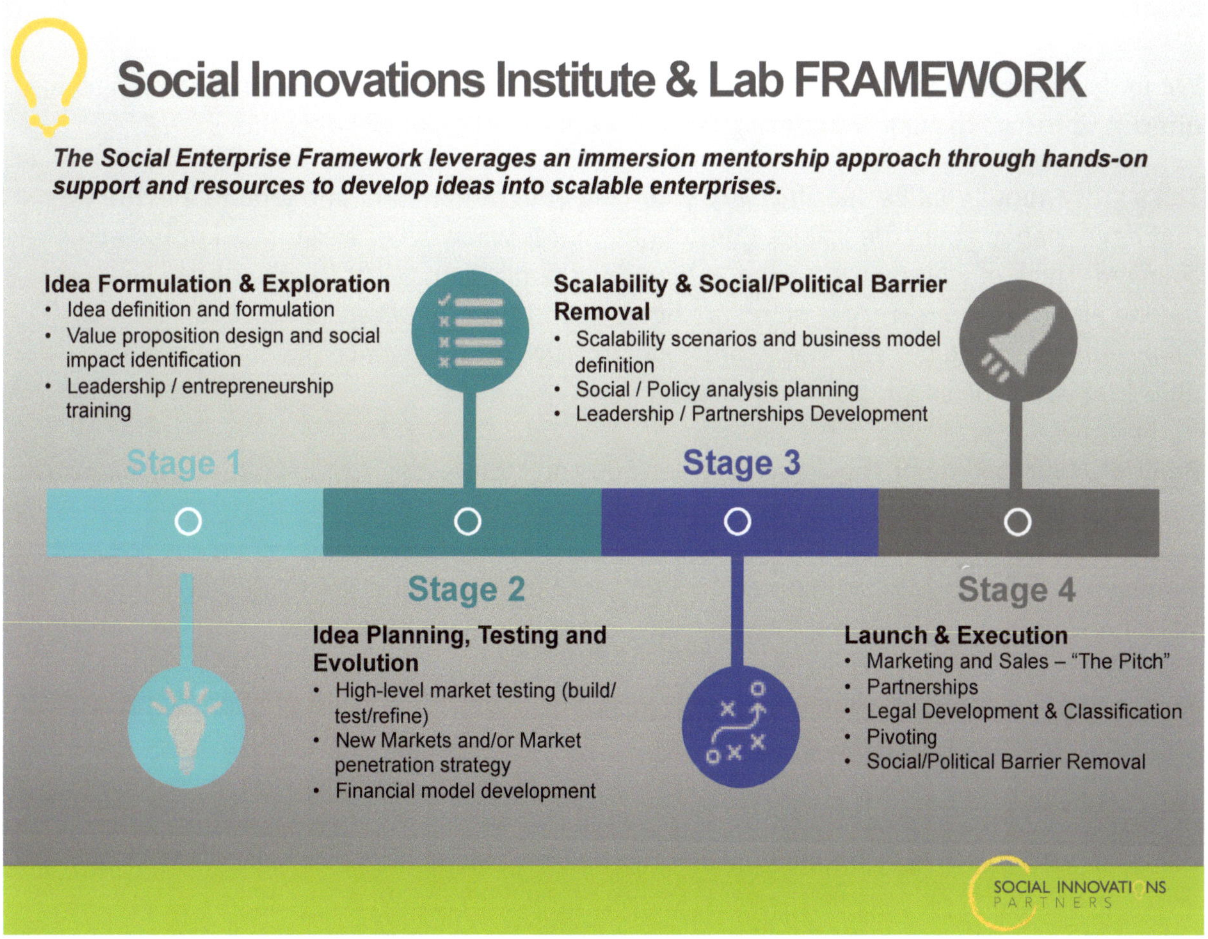

Social Innovations Institute & Lab FRAMEWORK

The Social Enterprise Framework leverages an immersion mentorship approach through hands-on support and resources to develop ideas into scalable enterprises.

Idea Formulation & Exploration
- Idea definition and formulation
- Value proposition design and social impact identification
- Leadership / entrepreneurship training

Scalability & Social/Political Barrier Removal
- Scalability scenarios and business model definition
- Social / Policy analysis planning
- Leadership / Partnerships Development

Stage 1

Stage 3

Stage 2

Idea Planning, Testing and Evolution
- High-level market testing (build/ test/refine)
- New Markets and/or Market penetration strategy
- Financial model development

Stage 4

Launch & Execution
- Marketing and Sales – "The Pitch"
- Partnerships
- Legal Development & Classification
- Pivoting
- Social/Political Barrier Removal

SOCIAL INNOVATI NS
PARTNERS

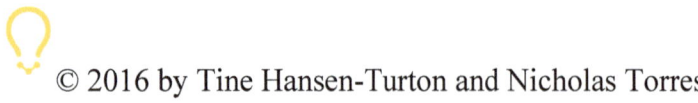

SOCIAL IMPACT: MISSION GOALS

WHY: TAPPING INTO YOUR VALUES AND PASSIONS

Complete your "This I Believe" essay: (http://thisibelieve.org/)

"This I Believe" is an international effort to engage people in writing about their core values and beliefs. The project is based on Edward R. Murrow's radio series from the 1950s.

We understand how challenging this is as it requires intense self-examination, and many find it difficult to begin. To guide you through this process, we offer these suggestions:

Tell a story about you: Be specific. Take your belief out of the ether and ground it in the events that have shaped your core values. Consider moments when belief was formed or tested or changed. Think of your own experience, work, and family, and tell of the things you know that no one else does. Your story need not be heart-warming or gut-wrenching—it can even be funny—but it should be *real*. Make sure your story ties to the essence of your daily life philosophy and the shaping of your beliefs.

Be brief: Your statement should be between 500 and 600 words. That's about three minutes when read aloud at your natural pace.

Name your belief: If you can't name it in a sentence or two, your essay might not be about belief. Also, rather than writing a list, consider focusing on one core belief.

Be positive: Write about what you do believe, not what you don't believe. Avoid statements of religious dogma, preaching, or editorializing.

Be personal: Make your essay about you; speak in the first person. Avoid speaking in the editorial "we." Tell a story from your own life; this is not an opinion piece about social ideals. Write in words and phrases that are comfortable for you to speak. We recommend you read your essay aloud to yourself several times, and each time edit it and simplify it until you find the words, tone, and story that truly echo your belief and the way you speak.

Edward R. Murrow said, "Never has the need for personal philosophies of this kind been so urgent." We would argue that the need is as great now as it was 60 years ago.

Watch Simon Sinek: (https://www.youtube.com/watch?v=sioZd3AxmnE)

1. What is the issue and social problem that you want to address?

2. In the section below, write your social impact goal (not your plan or approach) **STARTING WITH THE "WHY"** Include a section on what success would look like in concrete terms if you achieved your social impact goal.

The Golden Circle

WHAT
Every organization on the planet knows WHAT they do. These are products they sell or the services

HOW
Some organizations know HOW they do it. These are the things that make them special or set them apart from their competition.

WHY
Very few organizations know WHY they do what they do. WHY is not about making money. That's a result. WHY is a purpose, cause or belief. It's the very reason your organization exists.

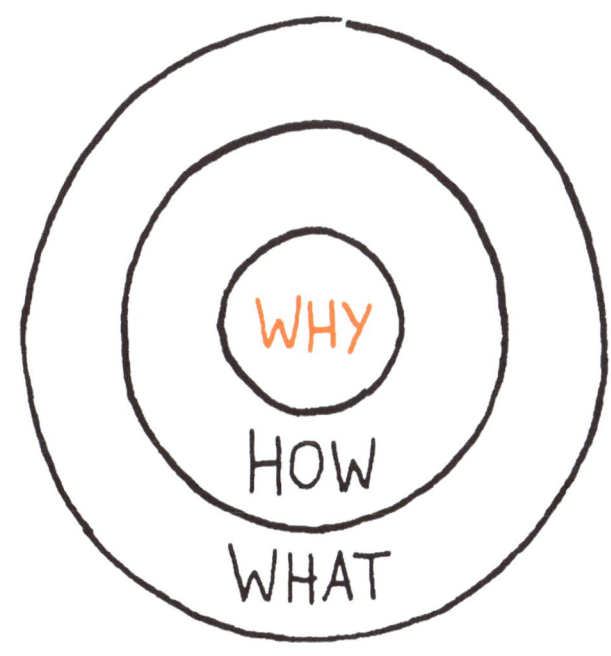

©2015 Simon Sinek, Inc.

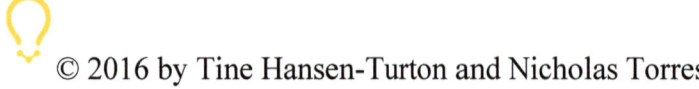

ASSIGNMENT 1: Write your "This I Believe" and "Why" Statement

Take the Personality Leadership Bird Test:

1. What Personality Bird Type are you?

2. How does this describe or not describe you?

3. What traits do you take from the other Personality Bird Types?

4. What are the strengths and weaknesses of each bird type?

5. How can you determine another person's personality bird type without them taking the test?

6. What strategy would you use to prepare a pitch to an Eagle, Peacock, Owl, and Dove?

Relationship-Oriented

Results-Oriented

Detail-Oriented

Relationship Strategies

How to Identify and Communicate with the Four Behavioral Styles

Leadership Bird Test Reflections

Compare your character traits with other successful Social Entrepreneurs.

"The Six Character Traits of Successful Social Entrepreneurs (from Bornstein, *How to Change the World*)"

1. What is your social impact goal (not your plan or approach)? Write a short essay on your social impact goal using your "This I Believe" essay as a foundation. Include a section on what success would look like if you achieved your social impact goal.

2. On a scale of 1 (lowest) to 10 (highest) what is your willingness to self-correct? Why do you give yourself this ranking?

3. On a scale of 1 (lowest) to 10 (highest) what is your willingness to share credit (a social entrepreneur's true intention is to make change happen, and sharing credit happens naturally through this process)? Why do you give yourself this ranking?

4. On a scale of 1 (lowest) to 10 (highest) what is your willingness to break free of established structures (constraints and bureaucracy in government and academia can hinder innovation, so many entrepreneurs either step outside these institutions or come from the citizen sector)? Why do you give yourself this ranking?

5. On a scale of 1 (lowest) to 10 (highest) what is your willingness to cross disciplinary boundaries (social entrepreneurs look for new ways to combine and use resources to achieve innovative, workable solutions to problems)? Why do you give yourself this ranking?

6. On a scale of 1 (lowest) to 10 (highest) what is your willingness to work quietly (entrepreneurs might spend years fine-tuning their ideas and influencing potential customers and stakeholders, with the understanding that recognition will come with time)? Why do you give yourself this ranking?

7. Describe your ethical impetus (entrepreneurs are focused on the why, with no choice but to do the work they do, and they refuse to readily accept that something cannot be done).

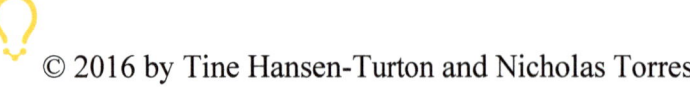

What Social Entrepreneur Characteristics describe and don't describe you?

DESIGN THINKING: WHAT and HOW

Opportunity and Innovation: Turning an Idea into a Social Model

Watch Clayton Christensen: Disruptive Innovation Explained:
(http://www.claytonchristensen.com/key-concepts)

Theory of Change: drives the entrepreneur/organization's purpose and process by identifying the population targeted for service, the outcomes and the program design. An effective theory of change should have meaning for stakeholders, be plausible and clearly state how the program will be delivered and its performance tracked.

Developing a successful strategy requires thinking about the big picture. A strong, plausible theory of change provides a template for focusing the organization's efforts.

What is the current status quo within your industry? Is your idea/innovation a *disruptive* or *sustainable* intervention/strategy? Describe how it will potentially disrupt your industry or innovate within your organization.

Social Enterprise Analysis: Case Study

Write an analysis based upon the case study given to you using the below questions as a framework.

1. Are you inspired by the idea? Do you believe the idea? Why or Why Not?
2. Does he/she have social impact goals or outcomes? Will their service/product achieve these goals?
3. Have they described the current industry status quo?
4. Does he/she have a Theory of Change?
5. Did they conduct a competitive analysis? Do they know what strategies have been developed/tried by others? Does their service/product take into account other potential or currently active competitors?
6. Did he/she consider the opportunity and timing for his/her idea/innovation?
7. Did he/she do any market testing with end consumers? How did they change their service/model based upon this feedback?

Describe your Social Innovation/Enterprise Idea.

1. What is your Idea or Theory of Change to achieve your social impact goals?

2. What is the product/service to be delivered? Describe, draw, create your prototype?

3. Describe and map the consumer flow journey of use/consumption of the service or product.

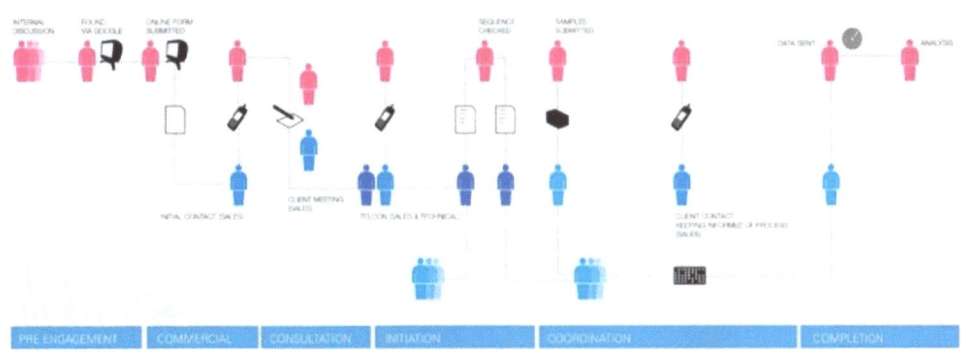

Is your innovation a Breakthrough, Sustaining or Disruptive Innovation?

((http://www.digitaltonto.com/2012/4-types-of-innovation-and-how-to-approach-them/)

Sustaining innovations are typically created by established firms, improve established products or services, and meet the demands of mainstream consumers. Disruptive innovations are often created by new firms, do not perform at the level of established products, tend to be smaller and cheaper to use, and have greater value to new/fringe customers. Breakthrough innovations involve a paradigm shift where the problem is well defined, but the path to the solution is unclear, usually because those involved in the domain have hit a wall.

Innovation Matrix

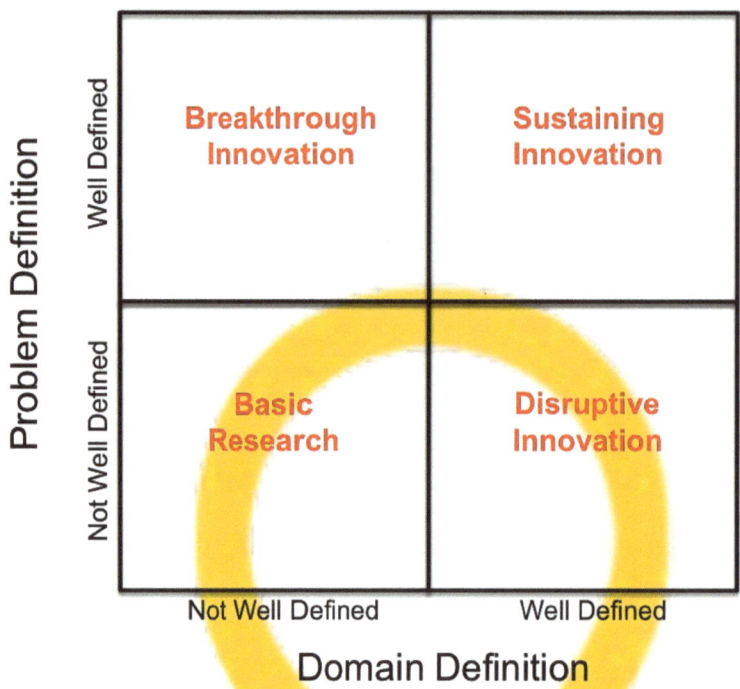

Problem Definition

Well Defined

Breakthrough Innovation	**Sustaining Innovation**
Basic Research	**Disruptive Innovation**

Not Well Defined

Not Well Defined | Well Defined

Domain Definition

4. What strategies have already been developed/tried by others? What successes were achieved and why? What failures resulted and why?

5. What is your value proposition and how do you know that your product/service has real value to the recipient (consumer)?

6. What is the opportunity and timing for the idea/innovation?

7. What type of market testing (rapid validation) do you need to do before developing a market for your product/service? When you do market research, consider that many people will tell you what you want to hear. Be sure to get to the root of what people want. Keep track of the assumptions you make as you develop ideas for your business or project, and update this list as you acquire new information and test the market. Note the source that allowed you to update your assumption (report, expert, etc.). Remember to revisit these early assumptions as you continue your work, as they may inform changes you need to make.

ASSIGNMENT 2: Describe your Social Innovation/Enterprise Idea.

Keep in Mind:

8. Social entrepreneurs identify problems that do not have an obvious or lucrative solution; if they did, firms would already be working in that area.
9. Social entrepreneurs need to create a market that did not exist before.
10. Social entrepreneurs work in areas that are uncertain by nature, thanks to new markets, volatile pricing, lack of governance, fragile infrastructure, new technology and/or unclear competition.

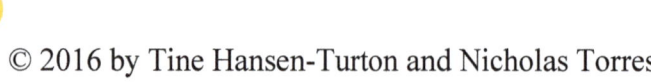

CONFIRMING the VALUE of your PRODUCT/SERVICE

Human Centered Problem Solving

Who is the target customer?

1. To whom are you not in business to serve? Who is your end consumer/customer? This is not your funding (government, foundation, third party payer, etc.)! You need to sell exactly what your customer wants. In the social sector, many third party payers, such as government, are not in touch with what the customer wants. If you can find people who would pay even a little for your idea, you know the service/product is real.
2. Describe a customer profile. What are the attributes of people who would be willing to adopt your service or program. Think about whether this audience is aware that they need your product, will see the link between your work and the outcome, how quickly they will see the benefit, and whether they must pay directly or the benefit will be funded for them.
3. What is the proposed value to the consumer? Think through the experience for your beneficiary. This is a crucial step, because the odds of success are low for social entrepreneurs unless you understand your end consumer.

Describe your target customer

What are your social outcome/impact goals (these should not be social outputs but outcomes or impact goals) and how will you measure them?

From David Hunter (*Evaluating Organizational Impact and Outcome Measurement*):

To be in the best possible position for funding social enterprises must develop and implement tools and systems to assess how well they are achieving their target outcomes. In the social enterprise sector, many organizations lack effective assessments for their programs and outcomes, but still expect to receive funding.

Outputs cannot be used to calculate social impact. Measuring outcomes is necessary and not as difficult as many organizations anticipate; the challenge is determining which data are needed and establishing an efficient, accurate system for collecting them. To quantify and confirm impact, outcomes must be directly attributable to an organization's program or service. The organization must be able to compare outcomes reached by those who received the service with groups that did not.

1. What are your social outcomes or impact goals? They must be measurable and you must be willing to be accountable to them.

2. What is the sequence of incremental changes that program participants/service recipients should pass through as they progress toward achieving the ultimate set of outcomes for which the organization or program is holding itself accountable?

3. Are you realistically able to measure your social outcomes or impact goals? If not, they should not be included in your final list.

4. Will you hold yourself publically accountable (via a dashboard) to achieve these social outcomes or social impact goals? If not, they should not be included in your final list.

5. What measurement tools will you use?

6. What scoreboard/dashboard template will you use to report your social outcomes or social impact successes?

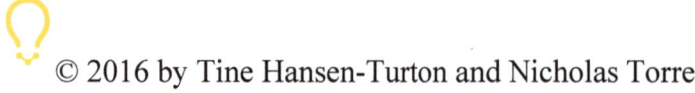

Describe your social outcome/impact goals and how you can measure them

What changes in your clients' lives do you expect to result from their participation in this program? These should be changes that are measured and monitored, sustained, linked to highly intentional staff efforts, and constitute what this program is held accountable for achieving.

Short term Outcomes: These are incremental changes that clients achieve in the course of their day to day program participation, and that can be thought of as "pathways" to the achievement of intermediate outcomes. New knowledge gained (e.g., knowledge of good parenting practices). New skills acquired (e.g., work readiness skills) and/or new behavior manifested (e.g., school attendance improved).

Intermediate Outcomes: These are critical changes that clients achieve at key points in their program participation, culminating with criteria for deciding they are ready to be discharged from services – namely, the conditions you view as necessary and sufficient to create a significantly higher likelihood that clients will, at specified timelines after discharge, achieve targeted long-term outcomes. Examples: Consistent use of good parenting practices, grade promotion annually, culminating in high school graduation, and transition from anti-social to pro-social peer group.

Long term Outcomes: These are the results of program participation that serve as the ultimate basis for assessing a program's value to society. Examples: Two years post program discharge, completion of an associate's degree program. One year post discharge, success in keeping a job with promotion opportunities. Two years post discharge, not having been arrested for criminal behavior over the post discharge interval.

SUSTAINABLITY

Financial Modeling, Attracting Capital and Social Return on Investment
(components taken/adapted from Social Entrepreneur's Playbook)

Develop your financial model.

Revenues
1. What are the projected sustainable revenue sources?
    - Making sales projections: observe customer behavior, use surveys, and observe any competitors.
    - Working capital: the amount of money you should have on hand for bills.
    - The more renewable revenue you have, for example from grants or consistent donors, the stronger your organization will be.
2. Who is currently getting the money for this service? How do you tap into this market, or are you trying to identify and create a new market?

Expenses
3. What are the product/service development (i.e. prototyping) and marketing costs?
    - While you don't need to know exact costs at the outset, you should do field research to make sure your assumptions are as accurate as possible. These assumptions will be the basis for your fixed/operating and variable costs, which you will use to make financial plans and estimate how much funding you will need.
    - If possible, avoid buying expensive, long-term assets during startup, which will deplete your funding and cause problems if your business does not succeed.
4. What are the product/service operational costs?

Financial Model
5. When is the model financially self-sustaining?
    - Break-even point: when the business transitions from losing money to making a profit, because you start meeting your costs through sales. Use this to pinpoint how much you must sell every month to cover your expenses.
    - Compare your total cost with your estimated income/revenue. Can you generate enough operating profit (or surplus, for a nonprofit) to cover operating costs, maintenance, AND loan and investor repayments?
    - For nonprofits: you should factor in a small surplus, above your expected costs, as a buffer against unexpected costs or market changes.
6. When does the model produce surpluses?
    - For long-run sustainability, a business must generate more cash than it spends. Consider these four places where you could produce a surplus, depending on the details of your project.

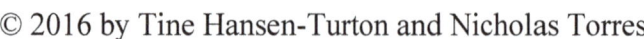

- Operating surplus: you bring in more funds than you spend on your general operations.
- Asset replacement surplus: charge yourself depreciation costs each year for assets including machinery, supplies, IT or vehicles that will eventually wear out and need to be replaced.
- Inventory and receivables surplus: you set aside funds to offset delays in cash flow while you wait for customers/beneficiaries to pay you (if you offer a physical product).
- Debt and investment servicing surplus: if you take out loans or have investments to eventually repay, set aside funds for interest rates or investment returns.

Start-Up Capital

7. Where will you get your start-up capital? Who provides the required seed capital (*e.g.,* angel investors, venture capitalists, foundations, loans, government, loans)?
    - Any **angel investor/venture capitalist** will want to know the logic behind your startup request. Equity investment: "angel investors" or "venture capitalists" invest money in high-growth, high-return businesses in return for a percentage of ownership. Because your success is uncertain, they expect a high return rate in order to balance the risk. A good investor typically offers experience, industry knowledge and connections. It is important to research potential investors and make sure they are a good match for you and your business – you could end up negotiating with them on major decisions.

      Keep in mind:
      - Show potential investors you can bootstrap. This is a lifestyle and mentality that shows investors you would use their money well. If you have a large line item in your plan for your own salary, investors will be less likely to trust your judgment. The importance of "bootstrapping" (financing some or all of your business yourself): you should make investments in your business, because it shows commitment to your mission and model.
      - Advisors can become investors, because they feel they have helped build your business. Be sure to talk with people you trust early on.
      - As the entrepreneur, you should be able to pitch and sell your idea in a compelling way. It is not sustainable to develop a business and scaling plan based primarily on who you will hire to do the work. Don't forget the human element in the face of innovation. There is money on the table to address issues of poverty and equality.

    - In the world of **foundations**, the first funder to support a new idea often gets a lot of credit; however, traditional foundations are typically unlikely to provide funding to create new nonprofits.

Keep in mind:
- It may be better to "piggyback" onto an existing nonprofit, so you can do your work while benefitting from their overhead.
- As a nonprofit, the "free money" you can get is counterbalanced by detailed grant reporting and accounting requirements.
- Nonprofits aren't able to scale (at least not initially) in the same way a business can.
- How to exist as a nonprofit-business hybrid: create two branches within your model, one nonprofit and one for-profit, then pay taxes on your for-profit work. This allows you to funnel funding and work opportunities to the appropriate area.

- When looking at public funding (**government**) opportunities, know that government moves very slowly. It is risk-averse and tends to have vendor relationships instead of formal partnerships. The Social Impact Bond movement attempts to change this culture, but its influence is currently limited (but growing).

- When considering **loans** consider:
  - Non-bank loans: nonprofits such as Accion and other entities have emerged to offer loans to socially minded startups, which can have difficulty securing formal loans from banks.
  - Bank loans and credit lines: typically require a business history, and as a startup it may be necessary to personally guarantee the loan or acquire a cosigner.

ASSIGNMENT 3: Describe your financial model (Revenues Sources and Amounts and Expenses Amounts for 3-5 years). Note your break even point and when profits pay back start-up costs.

Social Return on Investment (SROI)

If your business model is not able to demonstrate income and profits and you rely on philanthropic investments then you should have a Social Return of Investment Calculation to demonstrate the social return to society for their investment. This is also a good practice for initiatives that have financial income and profits.

Define your Social Return on Investment (SROI) calculations.
1. SROI calculations are important when seeking philanthropic and/or government investments AND when influencing policy.
2. Traditional ROI: how many times the investment is earned back by the investor.
    - Fails to account for social, environmental, or cultural benefits accrued by different stakeholders.
    - Monetization: calculating social value in monetary terms, to determine SROI.
3. Why analyze SROI?
    - Investment in the social enterprise is monetary, and the social impact should be measured in the same terms.
    - Can determine how significant the impact has been, relative to investments.
    - Improves decision making, communication, governance, and future investing.
4. How do I use SROI?
    - Valuation: how successful is the social innovation?
    - Monitoring: Have we met targets? Should we adjust strategy in order to achieve higher returns?

SROI Sequence

1. In concrete terms what is the social outcome of your social initiative? It has to be something you can measure.
2. What is the financial value of your outcome? Find a research study that indicates the value of your outcome. Cite the research study. If a research study does not exist then create a logical financial value.
3. Determine your success rate on how many people achieve the desired social outcome.
4. Determine how many people who would have achieved the outcome on their own.
5. Multiple your financial value of your outcome by the number of people who achieved the financial outcome.
6. Determine the number of years you take credit for the social impact
7. Subtract the amount of $ you spent achieving the financial outcome.

Write your Social Return on Investment Calculation

SOCIAL & POLITICAL ANALYSIS
SCALING and/or END GAME STRATEGY

Stanford Social Innovation Review: "What's Your Endgame?"
(http://www.ssireview.org/articles/entry/whats_your_endgame)

1. How big do you want to grow?
    - Evidence-based programs achieving social impact can plan to expand. In order to grow or replicate effectively, leaders must decide which aspects of the model will remain the same, and which will change. They need to think about the leadership, financial and organizational capabilities that must be in place.
    When establishing a nonprofit, the goal should be crafting a sustainable financial model during the planning stages. This will build a reliable revenue pipeline and help to secure and control the future.

2. Are there hazards of visibility?
    - Visibility: the price of success for your social enterprise. It helps you gain support but also inspires competition. In the world of social enterprise, competition is good for your beneficiaries because more people are helped as options and solutions increase.
    - Attention and intervention from authorities: as you grow, and especially as you disrupt existing structure and revenue streams, attitudes toward your business may change. You will likely attract attention from authorities, who may require you to file for permits or meet certain regulations that did not apply to you before.
    - Vested interests shift from tolerance to attention or obstruction: before you succeed, parties with a vested interest in your social impact area see you as a temporary annoyance. If you grow and begin to impact systems they use, they may create new processes for you to follow or policies that make success more difficult, such as increasing rent.
    Labor force shift from grateful to organized: in the early stages, people who work for you will be happy to have a job and make a social contribution. When you begin to succeed and scale, workers may start to organize, and will want to do better. This can result in your workers unionizing or organizing informally in ways that complicate your organization.

3. Are you straining your ecosystem?
    - When you expand, you may overburden your suppliers, which can hurt your product and beneficiaries. Pay attention to your suppliers and distributors.
    - As a start-up, you are in a position of weakness with distributors. When you grow, distributors may increase prices or impose minimum quantities.

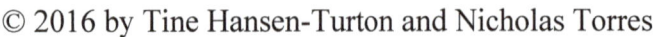
- Shift in beneficiary behavior: when you are new, beneficiaries are more willing to wait for the product. As you scale, they will raise their expectations and be less patient with you.
- Losing trained employees: you invest in your employees by training them, which in turn makes them more valuable to other employers. Competitors will recognize this and potentially seek out your employees.

4. What are your internal resource pressures?
   - Market shifts: as you scale, you will segment your beneficiaries and focus on the most important ones. Now you must balance helping your beneficiaries with generating the necessary revenue to sustain the business.
   - Production shifts: as you scale, your production challenge is sustaining your output and quality levels. With increased volume comes increased production and scaling up your scheduling and quality control processes, which requires trained management.
   - Financial shifts: when you grow, you will need additional liquid assets such as inventory, which puts you under cash flow pressure. It is important that your accounting staff know how to manage finances for a growing business.
   - Workforce shifts: you need additional people on staff as you scale, which may require more informed recruiting and training. Establish performance standards and have the discipline to train the best workers, as well as to let go those who cannot do the job.

5. What are your management challenges?
   - Management shifts: in the early stages you supervised everyone who worked for you. When you grow, you will start thinking about recruiting, training and supervising middle managers who perform well in your absence, as well as how to delegate tasks.
   - Moving away from the connected workforce: scaling and adding a tier of middle management removes the personal management style from earlier stages of the business. Create a strategy to move employees away from direct interaction with you and toward their new supervisors, so as not to diminish morale.
   - Conveying values: create messaging and communication channels that illustrate the values of your company and your expectations for employees.
   - Delegating: the demands on your time will increase as you scale. You have limited hours available for managing your organization, and should decide ahead of time which tasks to delegate to middle management.
   - Building finance and human resources: as you shift from doing most tasks yourself to scaling, you will need to develop departments to manage finances and human resources issues such as staffing, training and promotion.
   - Recruiting and training ahead: scaling requires formal systems for recruiting and training employees before you need them. If you wait to hire until the need is too great, you will be overburdened with training.

- Financial planning: scaling up calls for more strategic financial planning. Look at your funding needs and potential sources, and continue to avoid purchasing expensive assets that will unnecessarily increase your overhead.

6. Will you scale via influencing national, state, or local policy, consumer demand, and/or replication of the model?

7. Does scaling occur within the organization, through partnerships and affiliations, or through open source sharing?

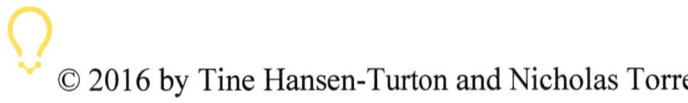

ASSIGNMENT 4: Describe your scaling and/or end game goals and strategy

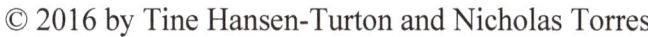

SOCIAL and POLITICAL BARRIERS
& POLICY/SYSTEMS CHANGE

Analyze social and political factors that could impact your model. Develop a strategy to address them.

1. Are there existing policies in place that will impact the design, reception or scale of this business model?
2. What are the social/political barriers and/or threats?
3. Who will my investors and supporters be? Do they have social or political interests at play?
4. Is the timing right to address social/political barriers and/or threats?

Three steps for identifying and addressing social and political considerations:

1. Identify stakeholders: your stakeholders are all of the people and organizations that will be impacted by your success, both positively and negatively. Think about their conflicts, potential reactions, and who you need to support you.
2. Categorize your stakeholders: allies, opponents, needed indifferents. Allies benefit from your product and might support you; you should determine which allies have influence in the market for your project, and mobilize them. Opponents will be negatively affected by your project; if any opponents have influence in your market you will need a strategy to address their concerns. Needed indifferents are people or organizations who are neither for nor against your project, but whose support or resources you may need (such as licenses or permits).
3. Develop a strategy: how will you engage your allies, manage opponents, and convert indifferents into supporters? Do you have the ability to influence these groups? If not, your project might not be viable in that location. Failing to account for your stakeholders will result in you wasting time, money and effort.
   - Identify the response you need from a given stakeholder.
   - What issues are currently holding that stakeholder's attention? Never assume that a stakeholder who understands you necessarily agrees with you.
   - Use your knowledge and skills: provide your allies with knowledge or capabilities that will help them (and hopefully grant you access to their allies); help an opponent with an issue to gain influence with them; and use your problem-solving skills to improve an indifferent's position on an important issue in exchange for their support of your project.
   - Do you have any physical or financial resources that could benefit your stakeholders, to reward allies or indifferents, and to win over opponents?
   - Use network connections – your allies and their allies – to mobilize supporters and help you manage opponents.
   - Find a "safe haven": this is the practical side of sociopolitics. You may need to identify a safe haven, or a protected position where you can launch your project without immediate or strong opposition.

- Create a diagram to map out your options for each stakeholder. Start with your strongest opponents, because if you cannot move beyond them, you may need to redesign or re-envision your project.

ASSIGNMENT 5: Identify and Map your competition and potential opponents. Describe your Social/Political Strategy to address social and political barriers.

EXECUTION

TAPPING INTO EXISTING MARKETS OR CREATING NEW ONES

Describe your strategy to penetrate the existing market or create a new one.

1. Is there an existing market for the innovation?
2. Brand identity is the personality of your business: it communicates who you are and why you exist, and it connects you with the interests and desires of your customers. Write down the characteristics that you believe your customer wants from your business, and key words you would use to describe your business. Do they align?
3. What is the demand? Do you have enough supply?
4. What is the marketing strategy and what marketing outlets will you use?
5. How will you build a relationship with your customer? How will you get them to know and trust you?
6. How will you get, keep and increase your customers over time? What is your price, and how will you sell your product or service?
7. List your key competitive factors; now list your competition's. Are they largely the same?
8. Are you prepared to fine-tune the message and market based upon rapid validation?
    o   Many emerging organizations pay special attention to social media and the web. These platforms provide low-cost opportunities to fundraise, make connections and promote the mission.
    o   A marketing strategy requires clear objectives. What should each communication accomplish – sharing the mission and benefit, highlighting a leader, marketing a new initiative internally?
    o   Cause marketing attracts individual donors, often on a smaller scale, by inspiring them to support a social issue or need.
    o   For efficiency, organizations that use social media for fundraising and cause marketing need to understand their audience. Finding the niche market for the program or service will help an organization reach its goals and raise awareness, with fewer time and financial commitments.
9. Blue Ocean Strategy (http://www.blueoceanstrategy.com/what-is-blue-ocean-strategy/) describes the process for creating new market space and building new demand. Blue Ocean Strategy focuses on establishing and working within uncontested market space, capitalizing on new demand, reducing costs and existing apart from competition. It is contrasted with the idea of the red ocean, which represents the traditional mindset around markets, competition and business strategy.

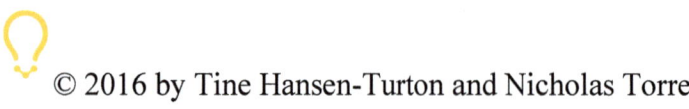

Describe your Market Penetration or Creating New Market Strategy

ORGANIZATIONAL COMPETITION AND PARTNERSHIPS

Analyze your competition, and identify your potential partners.
1. Who are the closest potential competitors? What is the most competitive alternative already out there (*i.e.,* who currently offers the best alternative approach to your product? Are you attempting to deliver a substantially superior experience, or something only slightly different from an existing alternative)?
2. Who/What is the competition? Government or nonprofit programs that subsidize a product or service you want to provide can also be competition.
3. How are you different? If your solution to the problem does not seem to match existing programs, ask yourself if you can create something that is substantially better. If not, it is better to abandon your project than waste time and resources.
4. Analyze the most competitive alternative: who are they and how do they market their product?
5. How have similar initiatives marketed themselves? Have they succeeded?
6. Who are my organizational partners? What value do they add?
7. What are the legal and financial implications for a collaboration or partnership? How do I build partnerships, and what partnership models do I use?

Types of partnerships:
- Collaboration: involves minimal integration, does not change any party's corporate or legal arrangements, and may not require any written agreements.
- Strategic Alliance: organizations reduce costs and maintain independence by deciding to operate certain programs together. One approach involves sharing administrative services, the other involves combining programs through a contract or other formal agreement.
- Corporate Integration: alters legal structure so that all parties can maximize their strengths and successes.
  - Management services: combines administrative functions
  - Joint venture: combines certain programmatic functions
  - Parent-subsidiary: combines both administrative and programmatic functions when a merger is not technically possible

Why do organizations merge?
- To **strengthen** existing compatible missions.
- To **increase** opportunities to assist in preserving critical community assets and extend programs offered by both organizations.
- To **enhance** financial stability and create economies of scale.
- To **strengthen** programmatic and infrastructure capacity.

- To **provide** new opportunities for career advancement for staff and enhance fringe benefits, as well as academic programs.

Describe your competition. List your partners and their value added.

LEADERSHIP & MANAGEMENT COMPETENCIES

Describe your personal strengths and weaknesses as a leader. Identify the members of your management team and their respective skills.

1. What are my core strengths? What skills and competencies do I need to compliment my core strengths? Remember the bird personality tests.
2. Do I have the right leadership, management depth, and skills/expertise to execute?
3. Who are the people on my management team? Do they have the skill set to deliver as individuals and as part of the team?
   - *Selling skills*: you or someone on your team should be a persuasive, effective salesperson who can secure the support you need while addressing and mitigating concerns potential customers and beneficiaries may have about your product or program.
   - *Operating skills*: a team member in charge of operations must be able to manage planning and scheduling while maintaining output and quality. An effective operations manager pays attention to detail at all stages of the process, always with an eye on quality.
   - *Accounting and cash management skills*: cash flow pressure is common in the start-up stages, even if the business is quickly succeeding and growing. When your demand is growing, you need to build up your inventory ahead of it.
   - *Negotiating skills*: there will be negotiations critical to launching your business, and if a negotiation fails it can damage your performance and potential for success.
     - When negotiating from a position of weakness, know what the worst possible deal for your business would be. You need to establish a line beyond which you walk away, otherwise you will concede and hurt your business.
     - Make sure both parties in the negotiation have clearly specified who is responsible for actions and activities as part of the deal.
   - During start-up, *avoid hiring full-time staff members*. Pay per task and create contracts until you are stable and successful enough to hire. Managers can be too expensive at the outset.
   - Everyone on your team should *know the break-even metrics*, and must be prepared to work harder as deadlines approach.
   - *Never compromise quality* in the early stages of your enterprise. If your first customers and beneficiaries – who have taken a risk in doing business with you – see you as unreliable or delivering a less than perfect product, your business may fail. When establishing a new product or service within a new market, it is helpful to spend time with your customers and establish criteria to determine the quality of your product.
   - *Don't forget morale.* When you meet a goal or achieve a marker of success, no matter how small, congratulate your team and share the good news.
   - Continue to *track and update your list of assumptions*, even as the business grows. It is easy to lose sight of these thoughts and ideas from the earliest stages, and end up relying on an initial assumption that proves to be false or misleading.

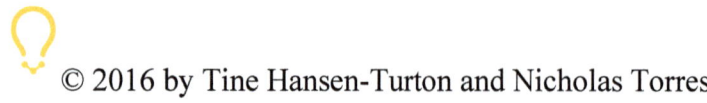

ASSIGNMENT 6: Describe your leadership strengths and weaknesses. Describe your management/leadership team and their respective skill sets.

MANAGING THE UPSIDE AND DOWNSIDES

Describe your strategy to adapt and pivot. How will you define failure?

Social enterprises are more likely to fail than to succeed, and it is important to know what failure means. Recognizing when things are not working is crucial, to avoid funneling additional money and time into your business.

1. *Define failure*. Before you launch, decide what failure means based on the minimal amount of revenue and delivered social impact in a certain timeframe. Below this marker, you would disengage from your business and devote your energies to a different project.
2. *Monitor sociopolitics*. Track your stakeholders, share positive impacts and refer to your strategy to watch and deal with negative impacts. The positive social impacts you achieve will help you mobilize allies and indifferents, and win over opponents.
3. *Preplan for disengagement*. If the project fails, plan out how you will disengage from it. While this process is counterintuitive, there is a high probability of failure and in the event of your exit, you want to leave your beneficiaries in the best possible position. If you fail, you should leave behind the smallest footprint you can.
4. *Monitor for second-order effects*. These are consequences, intended or not, of your business succeeding. The effects can be positive and helpful to society, or negative and employed by your opponents to justify their obstruction of your business.
5. *Redirect your project or launch a different one*. Even if you are motivated more by social good than by profit, looking for profitable ways to address social issues forces you to be careful about resources. In the event you cannot achieve a growth profit through your business, you may be able to operate as a self-sustaining nonprofit, or a nonprofit that has some revenue but needs occasional funding.

Describe your plans to adapt/pivot. Describe your failure criteria.

39

ENTITY TYPE AND OTHER LEGAL CONSIDERATIONS

Develop your incorporation strategy and be aware of legal requirements.
1. Keeping the law in mind: all businesses and social enterprises are responsible for following certain laws and regulations. Selecting your start-up entity type is one of the most important decisions you will make.
   - *Sole proprietorship:* you and your business are the same, with profits and losses reported via your individual tax return. You are liable for any debt or legal action. This structure is inexpensive but carries personal risk.
   - *Partnership:* two or more people own the business. Each makes contributions, and each shares in profits and losses.
     o General partnership: everything is equally divided unless specified otherwise in the partnership agreement.
       ▪ Pros: inexpensive to form, shared commitment, pooled resources, encourages complementary skill sets, joining the partnership can become an incentive for employees.
       ▪ Cons: shared liability, potential for disagreements among owners, shared profits, must pay self-employment tax.
     o Limited partnership: there are general partners and limited partners, who are protected from assuming personal risk and have little management authority; they are often paid a return on their investment.
     o Limited liability partnership: partners' personal assets cannot be used to satisfy debts and liabilities of the business. In some states, this type of agreement is only available to certain professions.
     o Limited liability company (LLC): protects owners from personal liability, because debts and legal claims are restricted to business assets only. LLC's are taxed at the individual level, so members report earnings on their personal tax returns. It requires additional legal work and more start-up costs than partnerships, but offers beneficial liability protections.
   - *Cooperative:* a group of people who decide to cooperate and work together to be more efficient and effective. Members have a common need, and agree to jointly address a need through one strategy; they vote equally and are responsible for making sure the cooperative functions.
     o Pros: fewer taxes, opportunities for government grants, group purchasing power, can exist even if membership grows or shrinks, democratic.
     o Cons: less attractive to investors because of members' equal voting rights, all members must participate and pull their weight for the business to operate.
   - *Corporations:*
     o C Corporation: controlled by a board of directors and owned by shareholders. A C Corp is a separate entity from its owners and is taxed accordingly. While it can raise capital from selling stock and is an attractive employment option, it is time-intensive, costly and complex to start a C Corp.

- o S Corporation: like a C Corp, operates separately from its owners and assumes all risk. However, taxes on profits and losses can be passed to shareholders. The S Corp has strict operating procedures and must compensate shareholders who perform services.
- *Social Entities:* combine aspects of nonprofits and other socially-minded businesses with those of for-profit businesses. The social mission is tied to the legal structure; however they are not recognized in every state.
  - o Low Profit Limited Liability Company (L3C): gives companies the flexibility to raise capital for social or charitable purposes while allowing them some profit to use as returns to investors. The IRS has issued very little guidance on tax obligations for L3C's.
  - o Benefit Corporation (B Corp): corporation created for a social or environmental reason.
- *Nonprofit and other tax-exempt organizations:* though filing for tax-exemption is a long and complicated process, this may be the best fit for certain types of businesses. Nonprofits follow specific rules about raising and using money that differ from for-profits. It is important to remember that for-profit businesses can have social missions.

2. A brief overview of other legal considerations related to starting a new entity:
- *Incorporation and licensing:* you may need to file paperwork with the state to register your business name and be legally recognized. Various licenses and permits may be required at the local, state, and/or national level depending on the nature of your businesses and product.
- *Intellectual property:* a means of legally recognizing new and unique ideas, inventions, or processes.
  - o Patent: protects an invention. Provisional patents can quickly help you claim your idea for a year at a lower cost while you go through the official patent process, which is expensive and takes time.
  - o Trademark: protects a brand, specifically words, names, symbols, sounds, and colors that differentiate goods and services sold by other companies.
  - o Copyright: protects a creative work, published or unpublished, such as literature, drama, music and art.
  - o Trade secret: protects confidential information, such as a formula, process, design, pattern or compilation. There is no filing required, but businesses must take care to limit access to the information it does not want disclosed.
- *Hiring staff:* you must follow legal procedures if you decide to hire. Consult the Small Business Administration for a full list of tasks to complete.
  - o You must obtain an Employer Identification Number (EIN) from the IRS, which is essentially a social security number for your business.
  - o Records for tax withholding: your employees must fill out W4 forms to be sent to the IRS, and submit W2 forms for each employee annually. Specific reporting requirements can vary by state.

- You must submit the form I-9, which verifies that employees are not working in the U.S. illegally.
- New Hire Reporting Program: employers must report new hires and rehires to a state directory.
- Workers' compensation insurance: businesses are obligated to carry this insurance, either through a private carrier, on a self-insured basis, or through the state workers' compensation insurance program.
- Required notices: employers must post notices in the workplace informing employees of their labor rights.
- Taxes: employers who pay wages are subject to income tax withholding, Social Security and Medicare.

3. Staying out of trouble: important practices for responsible managers.

- Separate personal and business expenses, even if you are a sole proprietor. This will allow you to track your funds, minimize trouble. Use a different bank account and credit card for your business, and pay yourself using this account as you can.
- If you set up any contracts or partnership agreements, ask a lawyer to review them. When you sign documents, be clear about whether you are signing as an individual or as a representative of your business.
- Get legal advice: talk to a lawyer, or ideally, ask a lawyer to be part of your advising team.
- Use a calendar to track deadlines and required government filings.

Describe your incorporation strategy.

MARKETING and THE PITCH

Develop a presentation to effectively market your business plan.
1. What is your particular presentation style and/or communication approach?
2. Start developing a pitch to attract interest and communicate your mission and model. Put the most important information right up front.
3. Use a story: it makes a personal connection and helps your listener like you. Be sure to use your own words and speak clearly.
4. Consider your audience. Are you pitching to potential investors? Are you trying to attract prospective customers?
5. Be concise, and practice to fine tune pacing and delivery.
6. Bring a product or demonstrate the service if you can. Use screenshots instead of relying on live technology.
7. Share what makes you unique.
8. Think ahead about potential questions, and be prepared to answer them.
9. Roadmap for planning your pitch: problem, customer, competition, solution, benefit, advantage, message, distribution, revenue, startup needs, costs.
10. A pitch is an opportunity to get good advice. Be sure to ask for feedback from anyone who declines to invest.
11. Incorporate details in your pitch that speak to your expertise, professionalism and credibility. As an entrepreneur, you are selling yourself along with your product.
12. Your slide presentation and other visuals should support your pitch, not be a crutch. Consider setting up automatic transition for your slides to keep your presentation moving forward and manage your pacing.
13. Think about the bottom line: measurable impact goes hand in hand with your altruism and desire to make a difference.

ASSIGNMENT 7: PULLING IT ALL TOGETHER
Write you business plan AND create your 5 minute pitch deck